W9-BYG-142

Key Bible Passages
Specially Paraphrased for Early Readers

With phonics
fundamentals
Reading Level 1

I Can Read God's Word

Phil A. Smouse

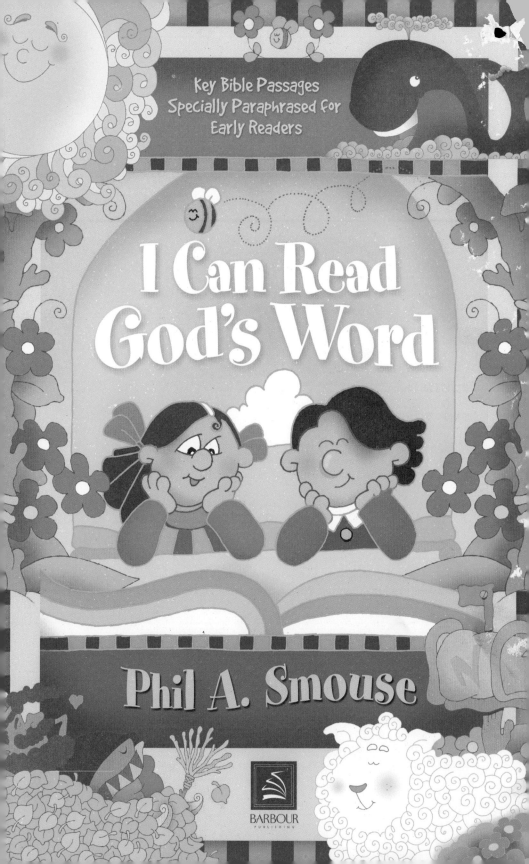

Key Bible Passages
Specially Paraphrased for
Early Readers

I Can Read
God's Word

Phil A. Smouse

BARBOUR
PUBLISHING

© 2008 by Phil A. Smouse

ISBN 978-1-60260-209-0

All rights reserved. No part of this publication may be reproduced
or transmitted for commercial purposes, except for brief quotations
in printed reviews, without written permission of the publisher.

All scripture quotations, unless otherwise indicated, are taken from
the New King James Version®. Copyright © 1982 by Thomas Nelson,
Inc. Used by permission. All rights reserved.

Scripture quotations marked NIV are taken from the HOLY BIBLE,
NEW INTERNATIONAL VERSION®. NIV®. Copyright © 1973, 1978,
1984 by International Bible Society. Used by permission of Zondervan.
All rights reserved.

Published by Barbour Publishing, Inc., P.O. Box 719, Uhrichsville, Ohio
44683, www.barbourbooks.com

*Our mission is to publish and distribute inspirational products
offering exceptional value and biblical encouragement to the masses.*

 Member of the
Evangelical Christian
Publishers Association

Printed in India.

Contents

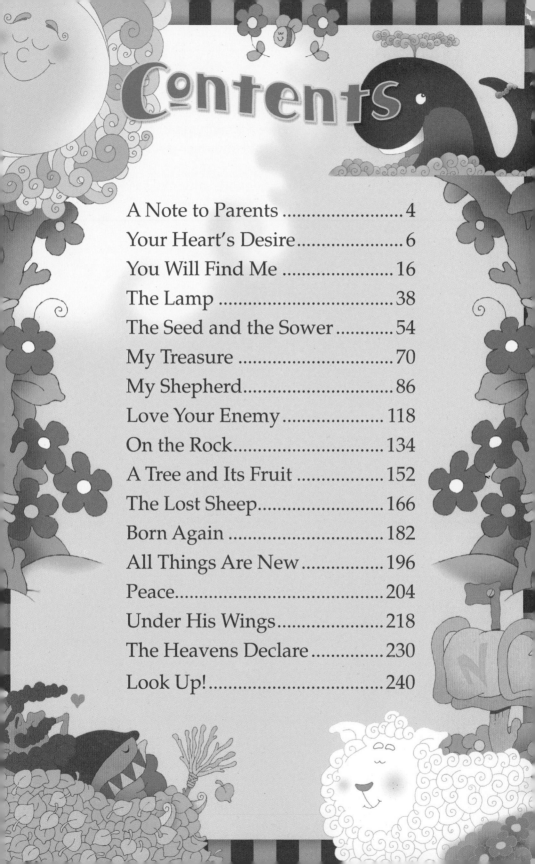

A note to Parents...

Thanks for choosing *I Can Read God's Word!*

Are you looking for a way to enhance the solid, phonics-based foundation you're building with your beginning reader? Then you've come to the right place. *I Can Read God's Word* is a practical, fun way to apply the phonics fundamentals your child is learning at home or in school to the reading of God's Word.

Let's Get Started!

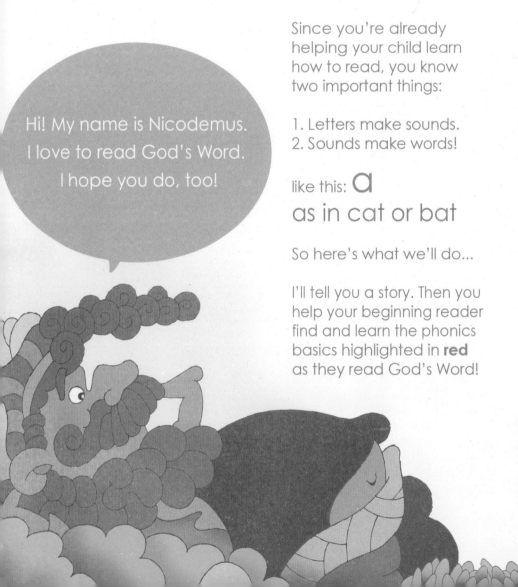

Hi! My name is Nicodemus. I love to read God's Word. I hope you do, too!

Since you're already helping your child learn how to read, you know two important things:

1. Letters make sounds.
2. Sounds make words!

like this: a
as in cat or bat

So here's what we'll do...

I'll tell you a story. Then you help your beginning reader find and learn the phonics basics highlighted in **red** as they read God's Word!

HERE'S HOW it WORKS

This is the story we're going to read.

It's followed by a brief devotional to help the message find its way into your child's heart.

Then a new word and its definition.

And finally the actual passage of scripture from the New King James Version.

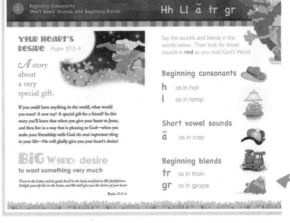

The sounds or blends used in the story are introduced here...

YOUR HEART'S DESIRE

Psalm 37:3–4

Trust the Lord and do good!

... and then highlighted in **red** as your child reads God's Word.

YOUR HEART'S DESIRE Psalm 37:3–4

A story about a very special gift

If you could have anything in the world, what would you want? A new toy? A special gift for a friend? In this story you'll learn that when you give your heart to Jesus, and then live in a way that is pleasing to God—when you make your friendship with God *the most important thing* in your life—He will gladly give you your heart's desire!

BiG WoRD: desire
to want something very much

Trust in the LORD, and do good; dwell in the land, and feed on His faithfulness. Delight yourself also in the LORD, and He shall give you the desires of your heart.

Psalm 37:3–4

Say the sounds and blends in the words below. Then look for those sounds in **red** as you read God's Word.

Beginning consonants

h   as in hat

l   as in lamp

Short vowel sounds

ă   as in cap

Beginning blends

tr   as in train

gr   as in grape

YOUR HEART'S DESIRE

Psalm 37:3–4

Trust the Lord
and do good!

Live and be happy.
You are God's child.

Make the Lord
your greatest joy,

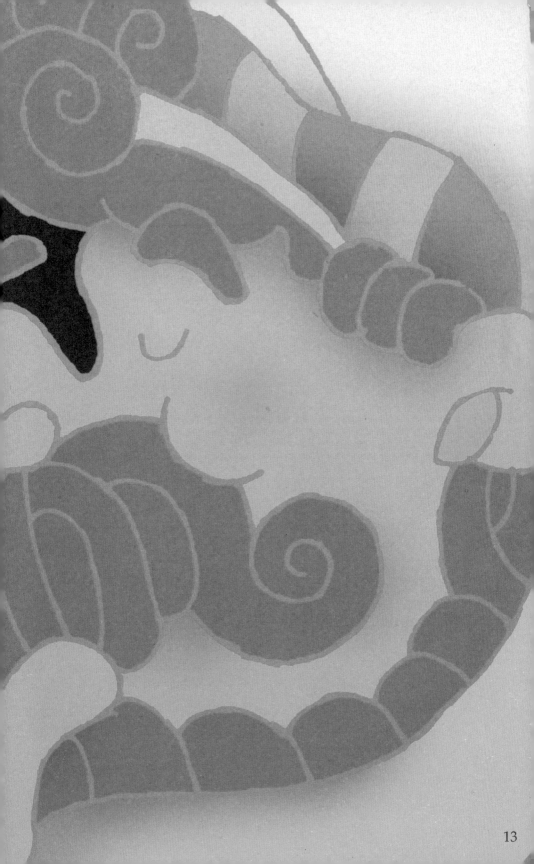

And He will give you
your heart's desire.

YOU WILL FIND ME Matthew 7:7–8

A story about wanting to be found

Do you like to play hide-and-seek? It's fun to hide. But it's even more fun to be found, isn't it? Did you know Jesus likes to be found, too? It's true! When we look for Him, we will find Him every time. When we ask for the things we need, He will give them with joy. And when we knock, Jesus will throw open the door to His heart and welcome us inside.

BiG WORD: seek

to look for something until it is found

"Ask, and it will be given to you; seek, and you will find; knock, and it will be opened to you. For everyone who asks receives, and he who seeks finds, and to him who knocks it will be opened."

Matthew 7:7–8

Say the sounds and blends in the words below. Then look for those sounds in **red** as you read God's Word.

Beginning consonants

j   as in jump

d   as in dog

Short vowel sounds

ĭ   as in dig

Ending blends

nd   as in hand

sk   as in desk

You Will Find Me

Matthew 7:7–8

Jesus said, "Ask."

"And it
will be given!"

"Seek."

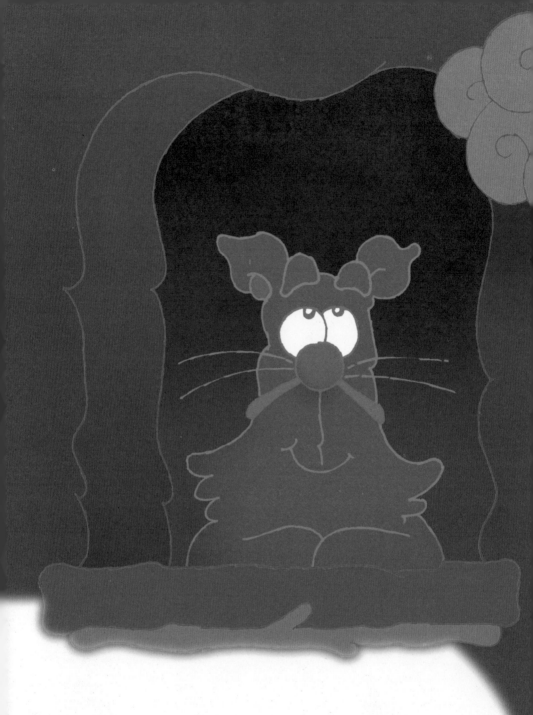

"And you will find!"

"Knock."

"And the **d**oor will open!"

"For every one who asks
will get what he needs."

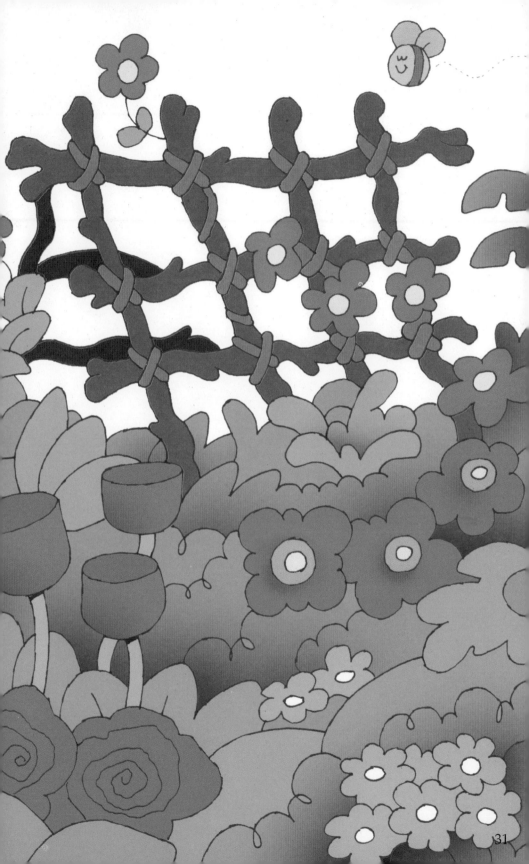

"Everyone who looks for Me will find Me."

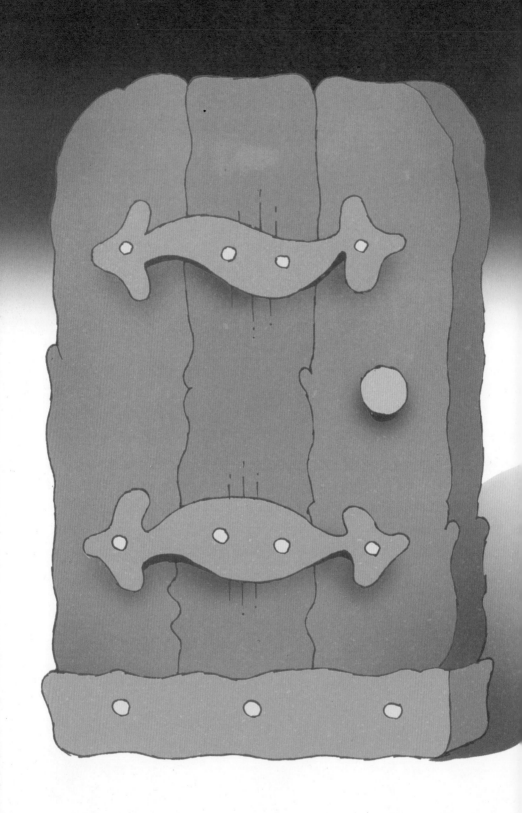

"And when you knock,
I will open the door."

"I will welcome you inside!"

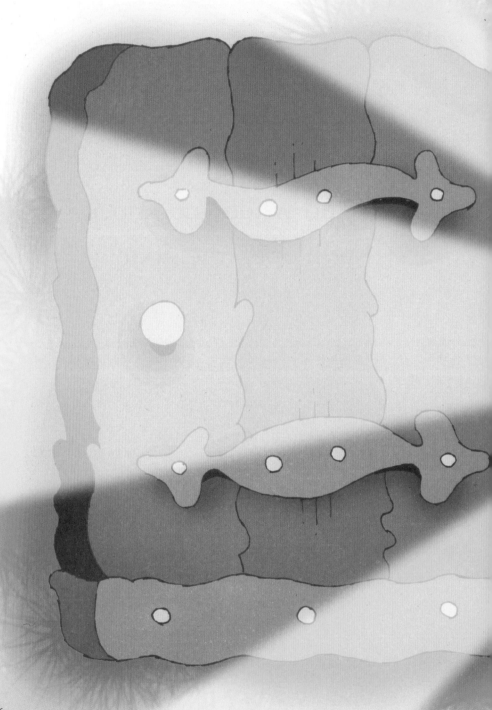

THE LAMP

Luke 8:16–17

A story about light

When you turn on the lights in a dark room, what happens? The darkness goes away ! There's never a fight. Light wins every time. Darkness cannot stay once the light has come. God's love is the light this dark world needs. So turn it on! Let your light shine. Share God's love with someone today.

BiG WORD: light
the power that makes it possible to see

"No one, when he has lit a lamp, covers it with a vessel or puts it under a bed, but sets it on a lampstand, that those who enter may see the light. For nothing is secret that will not be revealed, nor anything hidden that will not be known and come to light."

Luke 8:16–17

Say the sounds and blends in the words below. Then look for those sounds in **red** as you read God's Word.

Beginning consonants

b   as in bat

Short vowel sounds

ĕ   as in bed

Beginning blends

st   as in star

Ending blends

mp   as in jump

THE LAMP

Luke 8:16–17

Jesus said,

"When you light a lamp,
what do you do with it?"

"Do you hide it
in a bowl?"

"Do you put it under the bed?"

"No. You set it on a stand!"

"Then everyone
can see the light."

"Are you hiding
God's Word
deep down
in your heart?"

"Let it out!"

"Shine your light
so everyone can see!"

THE SEED AND THE SOWER

Matthew 13:3–8

A story about new life

In this story Jesus tells us about a farmer who went out to plant his seed. The seed that fell on good soil grew strong and tall. The seed that fell on poor soil did not grow at all! God wants to plant the seed of new life in your heart. What kind of soil will He find there? Is it hard and stony? Is it covered with weeds and thorns? Or is it soft and warm and ready to bring forth new life?

BiG WoRD: seed
the part of a plant that holds new life

"Behold, a sower went out to sow. And as he sowed, some seed fell by the wayside; and the birds came and devoured them. Some fell on stony places, where they did not have much earth; and they immediately sprang up because they had no depth of earth. But when the sun was up they were scorched, and because they had no root they withered away. And some fell among thorns, and the thorns sprang up and choked them. But others fell on good ground and yielded a crop: some a hundredfold, some sixty, some thirty."

Matthew 13:3–8

Say the sounds and blends in the words below. Then look for those sounds in **red** as you read God's Word.

Beginning consonants

f   as in fun

Short vowel sounds

ŭ   as in cup

Beginning blends

gr   as in grass

pl   as in play

55

THE SEED AND THE SOWER

Matthew 13:3–8

Jesus said,
"A farmer went out
to plant his seed."

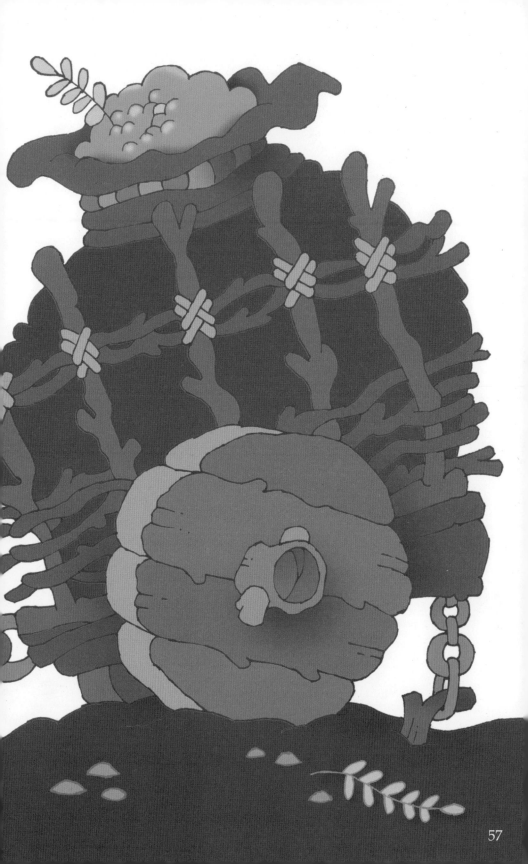

"As he spread the seed,
some fell on a path."

"But a bird
ate it all up!"

"Some fell on rocky ground."

"The soil was not very deep.
The plants grew quickly."

"But their roots were weak.
When the sun came up
the plants dried up in the heat."

"Some seed fell
in the weeds."

"But the weeds
choked the tiny
plants. Soon
they all died."

"But some seed fell
on good ground.

And those plants
grew,

and grew,"

"And GREW!

And they gave the farmer
a big crop. There were thirty. . .
sixty. . .even one hundred
times more than he had
planted!"

MY TREASURE

Matthew 6:19–21

A story about true riches

Do you like to collect things? Many things seem valuable at first. But when you look very close, you often find they're worth nothing at all. Others appear to be nothing but junk, yet turn out to be the most priceless treasures of all. What kind of treasure are you looking for? One that will end up in a mountain of trash or one worth seeking with all your heart?

BiG WoRD: treasure

something of great value or worth

"Do not lay up for yourselves treasures on earth, where moth and rust destroy and where thieves break in and steal; but lay up for yourselves treasures in heaven, where neither moth nor rust destroys and where thieves do not break in and steal. For where your treasure is, there your heart will be also."

Matthew 6:19–21

Say the sounds and blends in the words below. Then look for those sounds in **red** as you read God's Word.

Short vowel sounds

ŏ   as in dog

Beginning blends

tr   as in tree

st   as in story

pl   as in plant

Long vowel sounds

ā   as in pray

MY TREASURE

Matthew 6:19–21

Jesus said,
"Do not store
up treasure for
yourself in this life."

"That kind of **treasure** can be l**o**st for good."

"Or a thief may
take it all away."

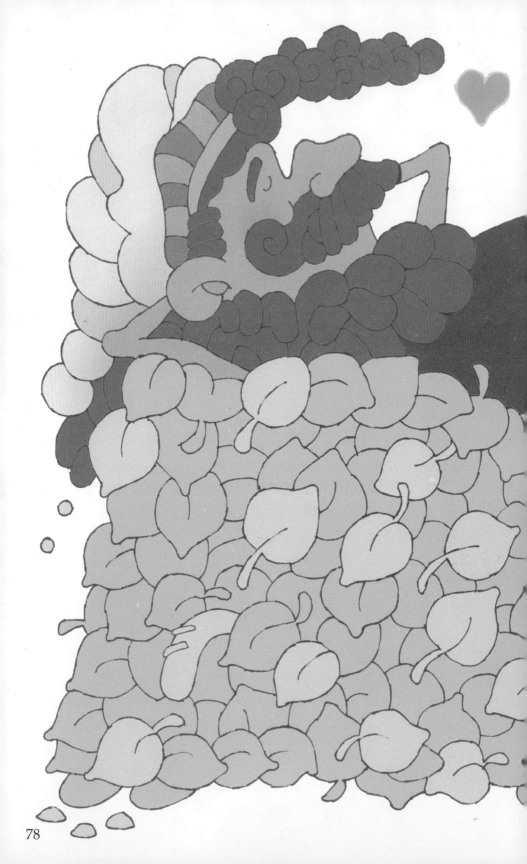

"So store up your treasure
with God in heaven."

"There it can not be lost."

"And no one
can take it away."

"For the place you hide your treasure is the very same place your *heart* will be kept as well."

MY SHEPHERD

Psalm 23

A story about forever

Sheep are funny creatures. They don't like to be alone. But time and time again they wander off and get into the worst kind of trouble! You and I are like that, aren't we? We both need a shepherd. Does that make God angry? Of course not! Jesus loves His sheep. He knows them by name. He will never leave you. His love is here to stay.

BiG WoRD: forever

for all time

The LORD is my shepherd; I shall not want. He makes me to lie down in green pastures; He leads me beside the still waters. He restores my soul; He leads me in the paths of righteousness for His name's sake. Yea, though I walk through the valley of the shadow of death, I will fear no evil; for You are with me; Your rod and Your staff, they comfort me. You prepare a table before me in the presence of my enemies; You anoint my head with oil; my cup runs over. Surely goodness and mercy shall follow me all the days of my life; and I will dwell in the house of the LORD forever.

Psalm 23

Say the sounds and blends in the words below. Then look for those sounds in **red** as you read God's Word.

Beginning consonants

m   as in moon

Ending blends

ft   as in raft

Combination sounds

sh   as in shirt

Silent e

e as in cake

MY SHEPHERD

Psalm 23

The Lord is
my shepherd.

I will always have
everything I need.

We will lie down in
the soft green grass.

We will walk
by quiet water.

God will give me peace
in my soul.

Because God loves me
He will lead me.

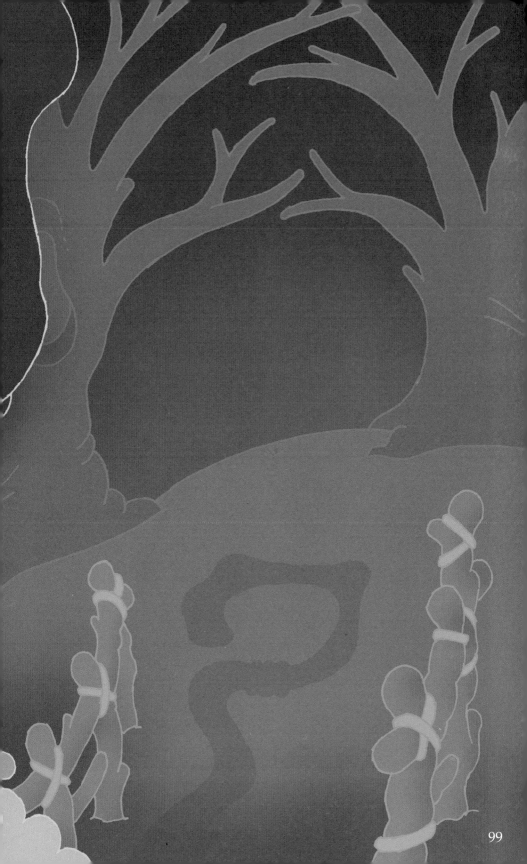

Even when I am in
a dark and scary
place I will not be afraid.
God is with me.

His rod will show me
where to walk.

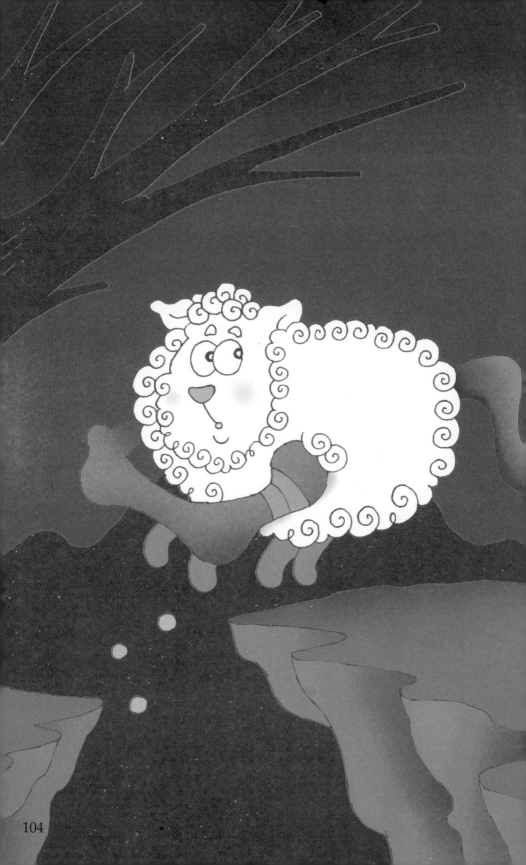

His staff will keep me safe.

His love will wipe
away my tears.

108

Enemies may be all around me.

But I will eat
in peace and safety.
I am the Lord's
welcome guest.

My cup will run over!

God's goodness
and love will be with me
every day of my life.

And I will live
in God's house
forever.

Love Your Enemy

Luke 6:27–31

A story about forgiveness

When someone tries to hurt you, how do you feel? Most of the time you want to hurt them back! Does that make things better? No. It only makes the other person want to hurt you more. Jesus says we don't have to live this way. It isn't easy. But it can be done. Are you having a hard time loving *your* enemies? Don't give up. Don't get angry. Don't get even. *Show them God's love!*

BiG WoRD: enemy

a person who wants to hurt or cause trouble for someone else

"Love your enemies, do good to those who hate you, bless those who curse you, and pray for those who spitefully use you. To him who strikes you on the one cheek, offer the other also. And from him who takes away your cloak, do not withhold your tunic either. Give to everyone who asks of you. And from him who takes away your goods do not ask them back. And just as you want men to do to you, you also do to them likewise."

Luke 6:27–31

Say the sounds and blends in the words below. Then look for those sounds in **red** as you read God's Word.

Short vowel sounds

ĭ   as in fish

Long vowel sounds

ō   as in boat

Beginning blends

pr   as in pretty

Combination sounds

ch   as in church

sh   as in shoe

119

LOVE YOUR ENEMY

Luke 6:27–31

Jesus said,

"Love your enemy."

"If he hates you,
be good to him."

"If he curses you,
be kind to him."

"If he hurts you,
pray for him."

"If he hits you on one cheek,
let him hit the other!"

"If he takes your coat,
do not stop him."

"Give him your shirt!"

"Whatever you
want him to
do to you. . ."

"You do that to him!"

ON THE ROCK
Matthew 7:24–27

A story about hearing and doing

Did you ever try to talk to someone who wasn't listening? Not much fun, is it? In this story Jesus tells us about two men. God was speaking to both. But only one of them was listening! God knew a storm was coming. So He warned both men. One man heard and got ready. The other did not—and lost everything he had!

BiG WORD: wise

able to tell what is right or true

"Therefore whoever hears these sayings of Mine, and does them, I will liken him to a wise man who built his house on the rock: and the rain descended, the floods came, and the winds blew and beat on that house; and it did not fall, for it was founded on the rock. But everyone who hears these sayings of Mine, and does not do them, will be like a foolish man who built his house on the sand: and the rain descended, the floods came, and the winds blew and beat on that house; and it fell. And great was its fall."

Matthew 7:24–27

Say the sounds and blends in the words below. Then look for those sounds in **red** as you read God's Word.

Beginning blends

br   as in brown

fl   as in flood

str   as in straw

Long vowel sounds

ā   as in rain

ē   as in ears

Letter combinations

oo   as in food

ON THE ROCK

Matthew 7:24–27

Jesus said, "If you hear my words, then do what I say. You will be like a wise man who built his house on a rock."

"The rain came down."

"The floodwater rose."

"A mighty wind
beat against his house."

"But his house did not fall!
It was built tall and strong
on the rock of God's Word."

INSURANCE POLICY

Fear not for I have redeemed you; I have called you by name; you are mine. When your pass through the waters, I will be with you; and when you pass through the rivers, they will not sweep over you. For I am the LORD, your God, and I love you.

ISAIAH 43:1-3

"But if you hear my words and do not do what I say, you are like a foolish man who built his house on sand."

"The rain came down.
The floodwater rose.
A mighty wind beat
against his house."

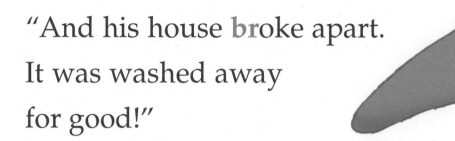

"And his house **br**oke apart.
It was washed away
for good!"

A Tree and its Fruit

Luke 6:43–45

A story
about
the heart

Do you know what an apple looks like? How about a peach or a pear, an orange or a lemon? Of course you do! They're easy to tell apart. But what about an apple tree or a peach tree, a pear tree or a lemon tree? At first glance they all look the same. How can you tell the difference? It's easy! Trees are like people. You have to get up close and look at the fruit!

BiG Word: heart

who you are deep down on the inside

"A good tree does not bear bad fruit, nor does a bad tree bear good fruit. For every tree is known by its own fruit. For men do not gather figs from thorns, nor do they gather grapes from a bramble bush. A good man out of the good treasure of his heart brings forth good; and an evil man out of the evil treasure of his heart brings forth evil. For out of the abundance of the heart his mouth speaks."

Luke 6:43–45

Say the sounds and blends in the words below. Then look for those sounds in **red** as you read God's Word.

Beginning blends

fr as in free

Long vowel sounds

ē as in bee

ō as in snow

Letter combinations

th as in thorns

153

A TREE AND ITS FRUIT

Luke 6:43–45

Jesus said,
"You will
know a tree
by its fruit!"

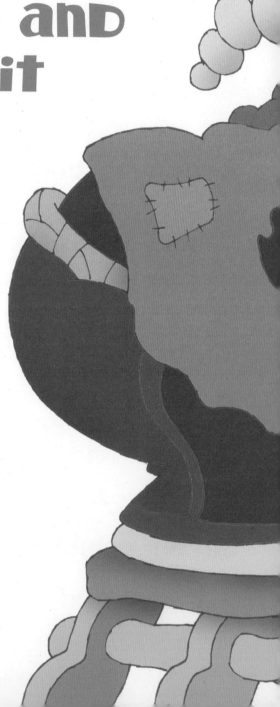

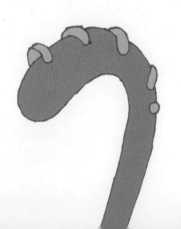

"A good tree
does not grow
bad fruit."

"And a bad tree
does not grow
good fruit!"

"Of course not!"

"So remember this. A good man does good **th**ings because *his* *heart* is good."

"An evil man does bad things because *his heart* is evil."

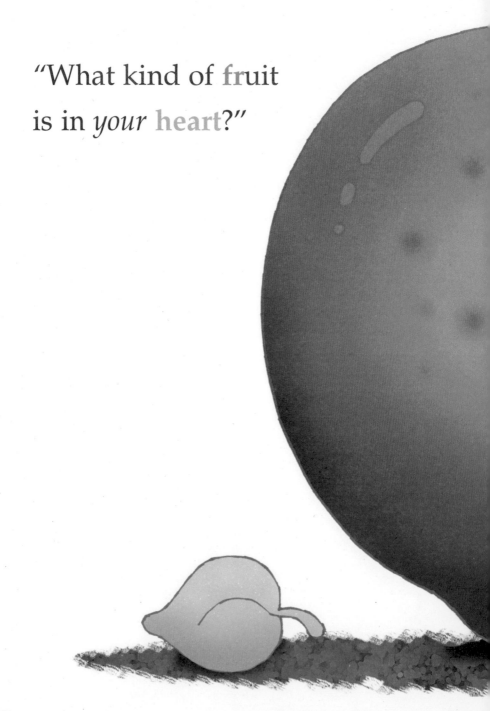

"What kind of fruit
is in *your* heart?"

THE LOST SHEEP
Matthew 18:12–13

A story about being found

Did you ever lose something very special? It's hard to think about anything else until you find it, isn't it? And once you *do* find it, oh the joy! Our hearts are like that. Jesus knows when we are close to Him. He knows when we've wandered far away. Is God upset when we lose our way? Yes! He wants us back more than *anything*. And He won't stop looking until we're safe in His arms again.

BiG WORD: lost
not able to be found for now

"If a man has a hundred sheep, and one of them goes astray, does he not leave the ninety-nine and go to the mountains to seek the one that is straying? And if he should find it, assuredly, I say to you, he rejoices more over that sheep than over the ninety-nine that did not go astray."

Matthew 18:12–13

Say the sounds and blends in the words below. Then look for those sounds in **red** as you read God's Word.

Beginning consonants

w   as in wink

r   as in red

Combination sounds

wh   as in white

Ending blends

st   as in rest

nd   as in sand

167

THE LOST SHEEP

Matthew 18:12–13

Jesus said,

"A man has a hundred sheep.

One of them runs away.

What will he do?"

169

"Will he leave
all the other sheep?
Will he go to find
the one that is lost?"

"He will!"

"But when he finds the lost sheep, what will he do?"

"Will he be angry?"

"No. He will shout for joy!"

179

"His little sheep was lost.
Now she is safe in his
arms again."

BORn AGain

John 3:3–7, 16–17

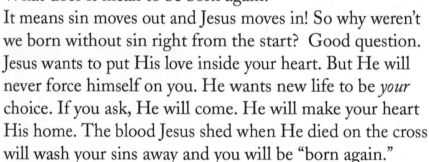

A story
about new life

What does it mean to be born again?
It means sin moves out and Jesus moves in! So why weren't
we born without sin right from the start? Good question.
Jesus wants to put His love inside your heart. But He will
never force himself on you. He wants new life to be *your*
choice. If you ask, He will come. He will make your heart
His home. The blood Jesus shed when He died on the cross
will wash your sins away and you will be "born again."

BiG WoRD: believe

to agree that something is the truth

*"Most assuredly, I say to you, unless one is born again, he cannot see the kingdom of God."
Nicodemus said to Him, "How can a man be born when he is old? Can he enter a second
time into his mother's womb and be born?" Jesus answered, "Most assuredly, I say to you,
unless one is born of water and the Spirit, he cannot enter the kingdom of God. That which
is born of the flesh is flesh, and that which is born of the Spirit is spirit. Do not marvel
that I said to you, 'You must be born again.' . . .For God so loved the world that He gave
His only begotten Son, that whoever believes in Him should not perish but have everlasting
life. For God did not send His Son into the world to condemn the world, but that the world
through Him might be saved."*

John 3:3–7, 16–17

Say the sounds and blends in the words below. Then look for those sounds in **red** as you read God's Word.

Beginning blends

sp   as in spend

Short vowel sounds

ă   as in cast

ŭ   as in sun

Combination sounds

ch   as in chips

Silent e

e   as in pine or cone

183

BORN AGAIN!

John 3:3–7, 16–17

Jesus said,
"You must be
born again!"

"But how?" a wise man asked.

"I will tell you!"
said Jesus.

"Long ago your mother gave birth to your *body*. You were born for the first time."

"God wants to give
you a *new* life
on the *inside.*
God wants His **Spirit**
to live deep down
inside your *heart."*

So. . .

"You must be born again! You must be God's child."

"Why are you surprised?"
Jesus asked the man.

God loved the world
so much He gave His
only Son. All who believe
in God's Son will never
die. They will live with
God in heaven.
Forever!"

ALL THINGS ARE NEW

2 Corinthians 5:17

A story about beginning again

Oops! Everyone makes mistakes now and then. But did you ever make a mess so big you knew you'd never, ever be able to clean it up on your own? Sin is like that. It's like a big, ugly stain that won't come out. What can wash away your sin? The way to get sin out is to let Jesus in! And when Jesus comes in, He doesn't just clean up. *He makes everything new!*

BiG WoRD: new

just made or changed for the better

Therefore, if anyone is in Christ, he is a new creation; old things have passed away; behold, all things have become new.

2 Corinthians 5:17

Say the sounds and blends in the words below. Then look for those sounds in **red** as you read God's Word.

Beginning blends

st   as in stone

Long vowel sounds

ī   as in pie

Combination sounds

th   as in thumb

Letter combinations

oo   as in boots

ALL THINGS ARE NEW

2 Corinthians 5:17

Jesus loves you.
He died to take
away your sins.

You can **st**art over right now.
The "old you" is gone.
Your sins are gone, **too**.

You are forgiven.
All things are new!

peace

Philippians 4:4–7

A story about being free

Peace is one thing everyone wants. But no one ever seems to have it! Why is it so hard to find peace? Because peace can only be found in one place. Do you know where to find it? I'll give you a clue. It can't be found some*where*. And it won't be found in some*thing*. Peace can only be found in *someone*. And that someone—*the only someone*—is Jesus!

BiG WORD: peace
freedom from trouble, worry, and fear

Rejoice in the Lord always. Again I will say, rejoice! Let your gentleness be known to all men. The Lord is at hand. Be anxious for nothing, but in everything by prayer and supplication, with thanksgiving, let your requests be made known to God; and the peace of God, which surpasses all understanding, will guard your hearts and minds through Christ Jesus.

Philippians 4:4–7

Say the sounds and blends in the words below. Then look for those sounds in **red** as you read God's Word.

Ending blends

nt   as in hunt

nd   as in pond

Combination sounds

th   as in thorns

Same sounds

oy   as in boy

oi   as in coins

Peace

Philippians 4:4–7

At all times,

in all things,
in every way,

rejoice!

Let your
heart be
filled
with
joy.

You do not need to worry.
God hears your prayers.

So tell God what you want.
Tell Him what you need.

Then give Him thanks!

And God's peace
will guard your heart
and mind because you
trust in Him!

UNDER HiS WiNGS

Psalm 91:1, 4, 14–16

A story about God's love and care

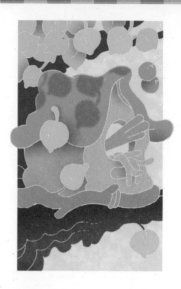

Did you ever meet someone who knows how to give a really good hug? It makes you feel wonderful, doesn't it? God's love is a lot like that. Once He gets hold of you, you don't ever want Him to let go. Are you cold and lonely today? Or are you happy, safe, and warm? Let Him wrap His loving arms around you right now. There's no better place you could ever be.

BiG WORD: safe
not likely to be hurt or lost

He who dwells in the secret place of the Most High shall abide under the shadow of the Almighty. . . . He shall cover you with His feathers, and under His wings you shall take refuge. . . . Because he has set his love upon Me, therefore I will deliver him. . . . He shall call upon Me, and I will answer him; I will be with him in trouble; "I will deliver him and honor him. With long life I will satisfy him, and show him My salvation."

Psalm 91:1, 4, 14–16

Say the sounds and blends in the words below. Then look for those sounds in **red** as you read God's Word.

Beginning blends

fr   as in frown

Long vowel sounds

ā   as in rain

Combination sounds

sh   as in sheep

wh   as in wheat

UNDER HIS WINGS

Psalm 91: 1, 4, 14–16

God loves me.
And I love Him!
His love has
set me free.

When I call Him
He will answer.

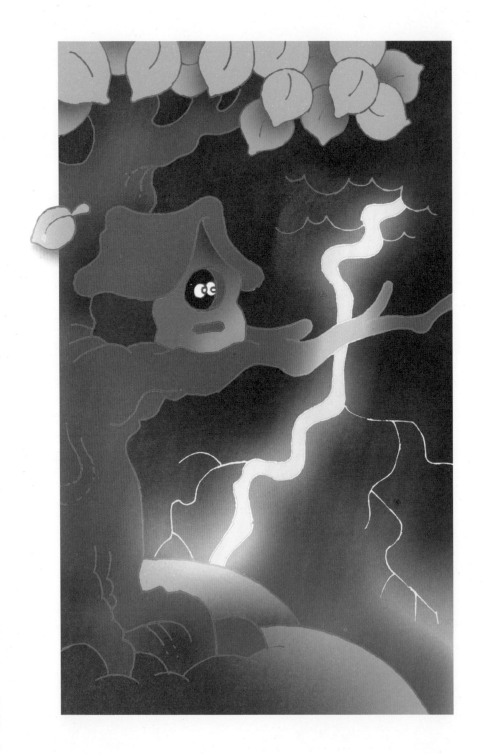

When I am afraid

He will comfort me.

I will make
my home
in the shelter
of God's shadow.

For I am **safe**
and happy
under His wings.

THE HEAVENS DECLARE

Psalm 19:1–4

A story about the beauty all around us

If the sky could talk, what would it say? If flowers had a voice, what song would they sing? The world God made is beautiful and full of amazing things. But did you ever ask, *"Why did God make all these beautiful things?"* That's a good question. And there's no easy answer. But maybe, just *maybe...* God loves you so much He made them *all* for you to enjoy!

BiG WoRD: declare

to say something important in a plain and clear way

The heavens declare the glory of God; and the firmament shows His handiwork. Day unto day utters speech, and night unto night reveals knowledge. There is no speech nor language where their voice is not heard. Their line has gone out through all the earth, and their words to the end of the world.

Psalm 19:1–4

Say the sounds and blends in the words below. Then look for those sounds in **red** as you read God's Word.

Beginning blends

gl as in glad

Long vowel sounds

ā as in pray

ā as in grey

ā as in train

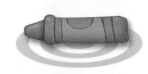

Combination sounds

wh as in whale

THE HEAVENS DECLARE!

Psalm 19:1–4

The heavens declare
the glory of God!

Day after day they speak
of His goodness.

Night after night
they sing praise to His name,

As God whispers,
"I love you"
all over the world!

LOOK UP!

Matthew 6:25–27

A story
about
trust

Do you ever worry? Of course you do! Everyone worries now and then. It's easy to get caught in that trap. What did Jesus say about worry? He said, *"Don't!"* Worry gives your mind permission to make your problems or troubles bigger than God. And that's nothing but a lie. So don't look down at your troubles any more. Turn around and *look up!*

BiG WORD: worry

to think about problems or troubles all the time

"Do not worry about your life, what you will eat or what you will drink; nor about your body, what you will put on. Is not life more than food and the body more than clothing? Look at the birds of the air, for they neither sow nor reap nor gather into barns; yet your heavenly Father feeds them. Are you not of more value than they?"

Matthew 6:25–27

Say the sounds and blends in the words below. Then look for those sounds in **red** as you read God's Word.

Beginning blends

cl	as in clock
pl	as in plug
tr	as in trunk

Long vowel sounds

ē	as in eat
ē	as in bee

Short vowel sounds

ŏ	as in log

L👀K UP!

Matthew 6:25–27

Jesus said,
"Do not worry
about the things
you need."

"You will always have good food to **eat**."

"You will always have
warm clothes to wear."

"Look up!
Do you see
the birds?"

"They do not work.
They cannot buy
or sell or trade."

"And they have
no **pl**ace to put anything
even if they could."

"But God feeds them.
He cares for them
just the same."

"So why do you **worry**?"

"God loves you
more than anything
else in the world!"

WRite to PHiL A. SMouSe!

Once upon a time, Phil A. Smouse wanted to be a scientist. But scientists don't get wonderful letters and pictures from friends like you. So Phil decided to draw and color instead! He and his wife have two children they love with all their heart.

Phil loves to tell kids like you all about Jesus. He would love to hear from you today!

You can send him an e-mail at: phil@philsmouse.com.

Or get out your markers and crayons and send a letter or a picture to:

Phil A. Smouse
Barbour Publishing, Inc.
PO Box 719
Uhrichsville, OH 44683